SUCCESS
Secrets
FOR
MOTIVATION

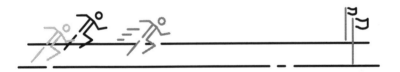

ALISON SHADRACK . CHRISTOPHER SIGMOND .
CLIVE DIGBY-JONES . GARETH MARTINDALE .
JANE THOMAS . JOHN LUNN . KEITH HOLDT .
MELANIE ATTWATER . NICK GRIFFITH .
OWEN O'MALLEY . ROBIN WINNETT

First published in Great Britain in 2023 by
Rethink Press (www.rethinkpress.com)

CONTENTS

FOREWORD

Motivation is a skill. That means it can be developed and honed. That also means it can become weaker if not practised consistently.

I am known as a highly motivated individual. I've received that feedback throughout my life and career. However, I would be lying if I said my motivation was ultra-high every single day. I've been very fortunate to have been trained by some of the world's top experts in motivation, the most significant of which has been Tony Robbins.

Tony's philosophy, processes and tools are, in my opinion, second to none, which is why he enjoys such a great reputation in the personal development industry. Sure, there are some who do not like his approach or style, or even his content. But I am living proof that when you apply yourself to positive change, you can become successful in life and business.

I started my own personal development journey and became aware of key skills, including motivation, more than twenty years ago. How does motivation affect my life today? I value it. Cherish it, even. I am nearly always aware of my own internal motivation (or 'state' as Tony calls it) and I can quickly move into a more resourceful and motivated state.

My work, as many people know, has involved helping people write great books about subjects that fill them with passion. When you begin any project from a place of passion, you have a good head start. However, big important projects – like writing a book – can bring up all kinds of fears and doubts, as well as practical obstacles and challenges.

It takes a certain level of commitment to bring yourself back to a motivated state and keep going despite these obstacles. Of course, it helps immensely to have a coach or mentor to guide you and keep you accountable, but it's unlikely that they would be by your side throughout every hour of your writing journey. Between coaching sessions, you need to do whatever it takes to maintain a motivated state to get that work done.

The authors who stepped forward to write chapters for this book deserve our utmost respect and support. Nearly every author has had personal or professional challenges which they have overcome to share their ideas, stories and tips for your benefit.

I asked them to talk about motivation, not as experts in that area, but from a personal point of view. It helps that they are all members of a very special business community called BIP100 (Business is Personal 100), of which I am also proud to be a member. The BIP100 community ethos values sharing at a very personal level, to help others as well as ourselves.

If the ideas in this book resonate with you the way I think they will, please do follow and connect with the authors. They are shining examples of motivation and proof of its power to create success.

Mindy Gibbins-Klein, International Speaker, Author and Award-Winning Entrepreneur

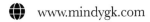 www.mindygk.com

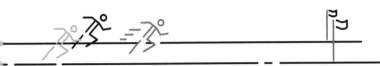

Motivation Comes Naturally When You Have A Clear And Strong Sense Of Purpose

MELANIE ATTWATER

When it comes to setting up your own business, this purpose comes from a passion for delivering a product or service which you strongly believe has value and will help people. For me, it comes from wanting to make a difference in my industry, and believing I can. I am a big believer in 'do for others as you want done for you' and my motivation comes from this – the desire to deliver a service and expertise that I myself would want. The desire to have an effect enables you to consistently have the willpower and energy to deliver.

You need a clear sense of purpose and belief that what you are offering is special – this is your unique selling point. To be successful, this should come from wanting to give. If your focus is about what you are going to get – money, reputation, fame – then I believe success, if any, will be short-lived. All of my business comes from recommendations – from clients telling others about the experience they have had with me when selling or buying property and my genuine desire to deliver service, with results and a lot of hard work and care, consistently.

When you are motivated, you are more likely to consistently work hard and be resilient and determined. Certainly, that is required in my industry, where I may have to rescue sales when a buyer pulls out or a mortgage is declined, etc. When you have a clear vision of what you want to achieve, it spurs you on. For me, this is knowing that I am helping people move on to their next chapter and caring for them through the process to minimise any stress. We all know that moving house is one of life's most stressful experiences – and sometimes this is also alongside bereavement or divorce. I find it so rewarding to know I am helping people in such an important period of their lives – it is a real privilege.

'It is well established that the process of moving house is one of life's most stressful occupations. That was expected when we chose to embark upon the sale of our house in Surrey and move to Devon. Melanie Attwater not only helped to realise a sale price exceeded by any other agent's valuation but was highly proactive during the whole process. Dependable, with constant communication at every point with *all* parties in the chain ensured the status was known in the full selling and buying timeline via WhatsApp 24/7. Cannot recommend highly enough; replaced the element of stress with confidence. Considering moving home? Melanie and colleagues will remove much of the cause of such traditional worry and concern.'

Graham Small, Client

So, what is your clear purpose and how do you break it down? Identify the specifics and the measurable and ask yourself if these are achievable. They should also be aligned with your values and beliefs as this will help you be consistent and feel rewarded in what you do. When you have a clear vision, you are more likely to stay focused and motivated, even when faced with obstacles and setbacks.

Another important factor in motivation is having a growth mindset and ensuring you have a positive environment. When you have a growth mindset, you are more likely to embrace challenges and view them as opportunities for growth and learning. I have proactively surrounded myself with a support network, including professional business coaches, other like-minded agents across the UK and the Business is Personal Networking Group.[1] I also read a lot of books and listen to podcasts to constantly keep learning. From new technologies and better practices to nutrition and wellbeing – I draw inspiration and support from all of these for my personal and professional growth.

Motivation is not a constant state. It fluctuates depending on a variety of factors, including stress, fatigue, external pressures or if you're having a 'bad day'. Knowing that you are continuing to learn and move forwards and that you have a support network is critical.

CASE STUDY: RESILIENCE

I believe a lot of my success comes down to the resilience I learned growing up. With quite an unstable background due to my parent's divorce and then my mother suffering from depression, I ended up spending a lot of time in and out of children's homes and foster care. It wasn't all bad – the children's home was affiliated with a Methodist church and this provided me with a community of really lovely people with strong values. On getting my A-level results, I was disappointed to learn I hadn't got the points I needed to go to Leeds University. Despite being told I needed to wait for the clearing process, I got myself on a train to see the Dean as I strongly believed I was capable of doing the degree – and I got in! I believe the strength to do this came from the resilience I had developed, as well as the values I had learned from being part of a good

---

1   Business is Personal, www.bip100.club

community. This all helped me build tenacity, which is a necessary ingredient for running a successful business. Graduating with Spanish and Business, I really didn't know what I wanted to do as a career, although I clearly had an entrepreneurial interest, having enjoyed setting up a small café business while on my year abroad in Peru.

My first job was in marine insurance, which I thoroughly enjoyed. However, with my love for interior design and Victorian architecture, I also started to do property renovations as a hobby and, alongside this, I ended up 'falling' into sales. I started off selling utilities behind a table in supermarkets, then moved to selling door-to-door and finally progressed to corporate sales. Certainly, the door-to-door experience helped me further in my resilience and sense of determination!

With my love for property and sales, I made the natural move into high-street estate agency, but I ended up frustrated at not being able to have control over the service I believed I could deliver. I joined a more personal, bespoke agency, which was a great foundation for me to believe I could do this myself. I then set up on my own as a self-employed agent, completely unaware that it was just a few months before Covid would hit the UK.

My decision to start on my own came from being motivated to deliver a level of service that I myself would want, helped by the determination and resilience I had learned growing up. That was my clear sense of purpose: knowing that I wanted to get up every morning and make a difference in my industry, to provide a personal service and to help people during one of their most stressful life experiences. A large part of this is being available, so I am online for my clients on WhatsApp from 7am until 10pm. I have learned, though, to try and balance my life and look after myself, so I take time out to go to the gym and keep fit.

The desire to help people has meant that all my business comes from recommendations. I value having an extended team – good solicitors, surveyors, mortgage advisers – with whom I host podcasts to give advice to people looking to move, as well as business coaches and like-minded agents offering a well needed support network to help others achieve their goals. I constantly listen to podcasts and read to help me continually improve and develop, both personally and professionally. This year I joined the Business is Personal community, which has been a very welcome support network for me, as well as a great environment to keep up to date with skills and find top-of-their-game experts, from digital marketing to artificial intelligence specialists.

Top Tips

There are so many tips I could give you, but I have decided on these three, all based on having that clear and strong sense of purpose, which fuels your motivation.

Firstly, have a clear offering, a unique selling point. What can you deliver that is different from your competitors? What value are you offering that sets you apart? How are you going to effectively communicate your offering to your target market? Can you demonstrate you understand your ideal customer and their needs? This will enable you to tailor your messaging and marketing efforts to resonate with and engage your market. Tied in with this is communicating your values. I invested a lot of time promoting who I am and what I offer on social media through Facebook videos showcasing properties, behind-the scenes, staging homes, etc, and this worked very effectively for me. People can see my genuine passion for what I do and the service I offer. I often have people contact me saying they have been watching me for two years on social media and now they are looking to use my service. This visibility helps build trust with clients. They feel they already know what I am about, and what I do differently. People want to do business with people they trust and whose values align with theirs. This will help you differentiate yourself and build loyalty and recommendations to support your business for years to come.

Secondly, and importantly, look after yourself. It is natural at the beginning of starting a business to fall into the trap of doing everything on your own, perhaps because of limited resources or not wanting to let go of tasks from fear of losing control. When you work hard to build a brand it is often hard to relinquish some control for fear of others not delivering the same standards as you. Ensure you have a strong support network both personally and professionally. Build structure and discipline into your daily routines, plan in 'me' time like some exercise and downtime to recuperate and have fun. Ultimately, taking care of your health is critical for your wellbeing, but also the success of your business.

Thirdly (and this is linked to looking after yourself) – choose your 'extended team' carefully. These are people who will encourage you, give honest feedback and be there to share the highs and lows. The extended team I work with and refer my clients to are photographers, mortgage advisers, conveyancers and surveyors – a network of people that all share the same values of providing personal, expert service. As well as this, I am part of the Business is Personal community and also have two business coaches. These provide me with encouragement, offer insights, expertise and guidance, and help me step away and have much needed 'balcony' time to review my business and look after the effect my work has on my health and personal life.

'We sold our house in Caterham through Melanie and team. They were strongly motivated from day one and moved at a stunning pace with the marketing and viewings. The photography was excellent. The house sold very quickly and they continued to track and drive progress to completion. And, importantly, they are all lovely people. Thank you, Melanie.'

Client

What is *your* motivation?

Melanie Attwater lives in Caterham, Surrey, with her ten-year-old son Lucca. Graduating in Business Studies and Spanish, she started her career in marine insurance. With a passion for renovating Victorian homes and experience in corporate sales, Melanie found herself making the natural move into estate agency. Driven by a desire to provide the best possible service and expertise, she started her own agency – quite a risk as a single mum and (unknowingly) months before Covid hit the UK!

Interests include astronomy, interior design and house music. She enjoys spending time watching her son play for Westerham Juniors football team, walking in the local North Downs woodland, as well as spending time in the Algarve, Portugal where she used to live and which she considers her second home.

🌐 www.melanieattwater.exp.uk.com

in www.linkedin.com/in/melanieattwater

f www.facebook.com/MelanieAPersonalEstateAgent

⊡ @melaniejayne2

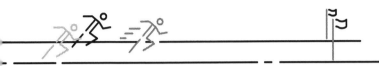

Motivation – Remove The 'Mote' From Thine Own 'I'

CLIVE DIGBY-JONES

Motivation is a potential battle until you become whole through a voyage of discovery.

Let's take a moment to think about my opening line. I could have said, 'Motivation is a natural flow of energy which powers us to achieve our goals.' However, the reality is that many entrepreneurs and others are suppressing parts of themselves to try to stay positive and motivated.

Are you looking for a few tips to try? Do you want to resolve the issue of living life at less than your full potential, however well you are doing?

Let me ask you a question. If being ten out of ten is being fully present – in a room, in your relationships, in your voice, your touch, your hug – on average, how close to ten are you?

Be honest. Some days it's an eight or nine. At times you may feel distracted and it's a five or six, or even a two. What is your average score at being present? Let's say it's six. That says that only 60% of you is trying to be a ten. That's a struggle, and you may be manufacturing motivation.

'I push myself.'

'On the one hand... On the other hand...'

'I have overcome x, y, z. I did a course and I cut off my negative thoughts and feelings.'

'I operate from a future possibility; I pull myself forwards.'

These are all examples of a split system. Have you heard of the rubber band effect? You leave something buried in your past and you stretch into a new future. At some point, the rubber band won't stretch any further and you can grind to a halt. Release the anchor from the past, including any past lives (if you believe in them) and you can come into full flow.

I ask large groups of businesspeople in a room, 'How many of you are, on average, at ten, nine, eight, seven, etc?' Occasionally, there's a joker who proudly claims to be at ten in terms of being present and fully motivated (until asked, 'What would your partner or your children say?'), but generally, they each discover that they are all at less than ten on the presence scale.

More interesting than the 60% of you in the present is the 40% of you missing or doing something else.

My stepdaughter, Sharon, read the book, *The Secret*,[2] and set about creating her vision of her future, even creating a vision board. She focused on it every day until she realised, 'As I worked towards my goal, I found that part of me was distracted, and it became more and more difficult to find the motivation to do the work.'

You will read in the chapters of this book about purpose, being powered by your heart, or steps to take, to feel motivated or to remove or change the things that make you demotivated. For me, many of these approaches are valuable parts of self-management. There are four stages in personal development:

1. Sleepwalking through life.

2. Becoming self-aware: Something's not right with me. I could be or do more. What caused it? What can I do about it?

3. Self-management: Part of me monitors myself and helps me improve myself, run my day-to-day, manages my mind, and more.

---

2   R Byrne, *The Secret* (Atria Books, November 2006)

4. Self-actualisation: Being fully integrated, whole, a fully radiating energy in form naturally triggering the Quantum Law of Attraction, having clear intentions and effortlessly magnetising people, resources and pathways. You can still meditate, do yoga, exercise, learn and grow, but be free of all the self-control.

Notice the SELF word. Let's talk about how this becomes fragmented and part withdraws, about inner conflict, and about acting out in the world.

Let's outline the Battle to be fully you, to remain fully motivated, plus how I and others found our missing parts of SELF and the fabulous results.

Become fully the Motivation, the flowing energy itself.

You have just discovered your Presence Score, out of ten. Why are you not at ten? If I said to you that at least 95% of the people in the world are operating at less than their full potential, would you agree?

If I said that there is an occurrence where we each may lose part of our Full Self and that it's common to everyone, whatever their origins, would you be interested? And if I said that there is a process for reclaiming the lost elements of your SELF, your energy, and moving to a state of full embodiment and being in the world, finding your missing Peace, would you begin to doubt my words and begin to judge me as some kind of metaphysical zealot?

My past, purely rational, self would have judged me too!

My clients are pioneers building legacies, seeking breakthrough. I am known as The Quantum Jockey. I have steered fast moving stallions and mares to achieve their goals and invent new futures and to achieve balance in life.

CASE STUDY: REINVENTION

I worked with the Chairman of a group who asked for help. In his personal exploration, he wanted a quick resolution, no deep work. With help, he was able to identify three opposing forces in him. Remnants of a twenty-eight-year-old super salesman, a forty-year-old creative leader of a choir and a five-year-old entrepreneur (who would run off with his 'toys' if he didn't get his own way). He was able to locate where in or around his body these stashes of energy were located.

Helping the energy expand, it flooded his body and then began to radiate out. He reported that his children barely recognised who he had become – a loving mentor whose warmth filled every place he went.

He was guided to create two mergers, and, with his business, he joined a global agency, becoming Group Vice-Chairman. He said, 'It was as if a brighter light was switched on in me and I became a beacon for change.' He watched as others lit up, just by being around him.

With clear intention, he attracted everything he needed and wanted, quietly being present, his energy magnetising. He had become vibrating, magnetic motivation.

CASE STUDY: I.N.B.E.D.

I was invited, with a colleague, to help a twenty-person team in Switzerland to introduce a new agricultural product into Russia within three years. It had previously taken twelve years and involved trading grain for other products and a large Politburo donation.

The twenty-person team was barely motivated. They came from different European countries, whose ancestors had killed each other across the ages, and they gathered in small groups each speaking their common language.

We used a process called I.N.B.E.D., developed after my study of Walt Disney and helping some forty industries, including Fortune 100 and 500 companies, to innovate. We had them **Invent** the new Russia that they wanted to sell into. They **Named** the symbol that represented the impossible nature of the task (in this case, the Berlin Wall). Then they **Built** a wheel using charts, with the rim of the wheel being aspects of the future world and the spokes being a line of charts moving from three years out back to the present, the hub of the wheel in the centre. It took a large ballroom!

Next, was **Enlighten** yourself (or your team). In a one-year leadership training that I conducted with a national retail group, it was this two-and-a-half-hour session with each participant that they said made the difference. Similarly with this group. Twenty individual sessions to find and release blocks to performance, belief systems, and delivering on their life purpose. Now we had a team. The meeting when they first regrouped was electric, emotional and real.

Finally, **Do** it now/Act as if. They started to behave as if the new world existed, and the Russians responded positively.

Before Glasnost and Perestroika, in 1986, new bridges were created and relationships built.

Three years to the day in December 1989, the Berlin Wall was breached and their product launched. Was this good planning, good luck or inventing the future (while releasing the inner world)? The motivation was innate.

So, why are we not all at ten out of ten?

What is fragmentation of energy? How is it relevant?

Simply put, we are made of energy at the quantum level. We come into form and radiate outwards. This radiance, as a baby, attracts what we need – food, love, caring. The absence of our needs (or physical/mental/emotional hurt) has our radiance withdraw and, if severe enough, the energy implodes and fragments, and may explode. The rest of the person continues. The process may repeat itself.

Clinical studies show that the withdrawn energy/consciousness continues to exist and signals its negative experience through a variety of negative feelings, which plague us. We learn to suppress the feelings and, eventually, they can cause ill health and we may act out with negativity and even violence. Beyond genetics, is energenetics.

What has this got to do with motivation?

This inner conflict as stored energy is fuelling distraction. So, rather than focusing on the symptom and needing to manufacture motivation, go to the cause and find and release your missing energy, creating free-flowing natural magnetism and drive.

One of the books I am writing is *Putting Humpty Dumpty Together Again*. My personal story. It contains a poem I wrote about my partner, Dr. Eileen Watkins Seymour's work – RAPSI® (the Ravenscroft Approach to Psycho-Spiritual Integration), which I have experienced, learned and teach.

Queen RAPSI®

All the King's horses and all the King's men couldn't put Humpty together again!

The King was distraught, Queen RAPSI® was not!

She gathered the pieces unheeded.

And although there's a mess, I can see deep inside that it's light that's desperately needed.

She helped him explore, as Humpty awoke, and the hurt and the cracks receded.

The magic was working, light shone all around.

Once again, Queen RAPSI® succeeded.

Top Tips

Here are three things I suggest you consider:

1. Recognise that, on average, however you measure your success, you are not fully present and that your motivation may be partially engineered.

2. Work with a coach or RAPSI® trained psychologist to help you map and locate your missing energy/SELF.

3. Shift from looking outside yourself for answers. Rather than trying to raise your vibration, gather all your inner and outer energies and fully embody and radiate them, becoming a whole, empowered being, in tune with the Quantum Law of Attraction. Then, 'Intention' is the key.

Self-motivation becomes an irrelevance. Motivation is now full energy.

Clive Digby-Jones is an Author, International Innovation Consultant, Executive/Board Coach, known as The Quantum Jockey, with thirty+ years in business to CEO and Group Board level. Clive conducted the study of Walt Disney's management of creativity for Disney University and guided forty+ industries, Fortune 500 companies to solopreneurs, in New World breakthroughs. He lectures on Creating Real Change and, with his partner Dr. Eileen Watkins Seymour DSc HC, has created the RAPSI® Institute to transmit their proven inner change process, globally. His latest venture is co-founding and directing Global Wellness Transformation, building wellness and conscious wealth.

in www.linkedin.com/in/clive-digby-jones-the-quantum-jockey

🌐 www.globalwellnesstransformation.com

🌐 www.ravenscroft.com

✉ clive@thequantumjockey.com

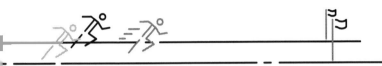

Motivation Is The Depth And Meaning Of Your Why

NICK GRIFFITH

Have you ever struggled with motivation and wondered how other people seem to tap into infinite pools of focus and motivation? From sports people, to people overcoming a disability – they are all around.

How do they find the motivation to keep going in the face of real adversity, when many of us seem to struggle with motivation?

They have tapped into something we all have when we need it.

When the WHY is big enough, you will find the motivation.

The deeper the WHY, the greater your motivation.

When you are struggling for motivation on a task, go deeper on the 'why' and think about all the people this will affect – from your family, your parents, your friends, your business, your employees, your community, the planet. The collective why becomes a much bigger motivated force.

Think about what you are doing and what it will mean to everyone.

What will it mean to them if you don't do it? What could they miss out on, which they will never know about, but which could have changed things massively?

Look at all the angles. Consider what impact your actions could have on all the people (and all of life).

Finding motivation is all about finding real depth and meaning to your WHY. Once you're aligned and it's tapped in, you will find real power.

For me, life events pushed me to find new power and motivation in my whys and meaning. My challenge was for life or death.

When I was thirty years old, I was struck down with encephalitis. I was having seizures every twenty minutes.

They put me into a coma for six weeks and I spent ten days in ICU on the edge of life and death.

I had entered a spirit state – I was looking down at myself in a hospital bed – floating above and not seeing anything other than a light with a rope towards it. The rest was darkness. I decided that I was going towards the light – it was the only way I was coming back, because I knew my time wasn't done.

My 'why' was simple, but powerful – life or death – and I was 100% motivated! When I reached the light at the end of the rope, I sat upright in the hospital bed. I didn't know my name, who I was, or who my parents were.

I was going to find a way out of this. I didn't know how, but I knew I would.

The doctors said they had never seen anyone walk out of hospital after suffering what I had been through. There was no manual on what happens next, so I wrote one. I rebuilt my memory and life from scratch. I problem-solved my way out because I was so motivated.

I was feeling the most motivated I had ever felt in my life. A life and death experience showed me the power and determination we all have available in infinite resources when the why is *really* big and *really* means something to people.

Now I understand the people who seem to have infinite motivation.

Businesses large and small look to create brands that identify them as good for customers, good for staff, good for community, good for charity, good for the planet – they are all trying to increase their WHYs to motivate you more.

Now, go and write down a list of everything you are struggling with on motivation. For each, really think really hard about the people you are doing this for and all the reasons why you are doing it.

CASE STUDY: MY JOURNEY RAISING THE STAKES

While getting my Master's Degree in Mechanical Engineering, I also co-created the inaugural Imperial College Summer Ball, which attracted over 800 people to Alexandra Palace. I was the headlining DJ, so I had to choose the right music to get the crowd going.

This whole event taught me the importance of understanding your target market and their likes and dislikes.

I discovered that the higher the stakes, the more motivated I became to succeed and the better problem-solver I became when I was pushing my abilities.

Once you commit yourself to do something personally, or start with a new client, or commit to anything new (especially if you're not sure exactly how you will do it), you will find new motivation.

You will find yourself in a newly motivated state — perhaps with drive coming out of new fears of failure, or embarrassment. It is good to stretch beyond your perceived limits, both personally and in business. You will find you reach new heights.

I was always passionate and motivated to use the power of people and networking. Joint ventures will always offer huge opportunities to every business when they are executed well. With one client, I had to fill the O2 London for a three-day business show featuring Richard Branson. I created the JV deal that allowed speakers to present on stage in return for promoting the event. Six weeks later, our list had grown by 30,000 and 7,500 attendees turned up.

I also created JV Dinners, which was a VIP networking event for business owners who each had their own large lists. JV Dinners not only helped me find new clients; most importantly, it helped all my guests to network in a high-calibre crowd. Everyone was highly motivated to attend because I was providing something they wanted. Nobody else was.

Leverage the power of your network through personal networking (keeping in touch and attending events) and keep an eye out for JV opportunities when there are clear win-wins.

I created the Digital Marketing Partnership as a digital agency which works with clients over the long term to get better results. One area I focus on with clients is improving engagement. I think engagement comes when people are motivated to click, read, listen or watch to learn more. For example, people engage with scorecard quizzes if they are curious and motivated to find more. Here's a couple of scorecards I've built for clients:

- Which area of business is holding you back from growing quickly? (Mac Attram)

- How ready are you to write your book? (*The Book Midwife* by Mindy Gibbins-Klein)

As well as building scorecard quizzes, I also manage their ongoing performance. Some clients see enquiry rates over 25%, which is high when you consider that 5% is good for a normal landing page.

I have seen the more you personalise the follow-up and segment their content based on their preferences, the more motivated they become towards following your brand and buying. The data you gather also helps you to gain more insights on your audience, which can help you improve your products and service and run better targeted ads in the future.

I am also motivated by learning new things. In 2023, I co-created Imperial AI Ltd with an old uni friend; we help businesses create AI-Powered Tools which increase growth and maximise cost savings. I am on a personal mission to try and bring the best parts of AI into business so businesses of all sizes can use the technology and get the benefits.

Top Tips

Tip 1: Dive deep

Do you want to find more motivation? Consider all the people affected by your decisions and actions. Take time to contemplate the impact your choices will have on all the people in your life, including your family, friends, employees, community and beyond.

As you pursue your goals, don't limit yourself to just financial targets. While these targets are important, they don't tap into the deeper emotional aspects driving your motivation. Instead, dive into the emotions and desires that fuel your ambitions, both personally and professionally. Reflect on all the lives you'll impact with your results, the opportunities you'll create, and the positive changes you can bring about.

By understanding the significance of your actions on others, you will foster a deeper sense of purpose and motivation that inspires you to go for success and make a lasting, positive impact. In running your business, think about all the people your business impacts, such as your customers, your staff and their families and your community. By keeping all of them at the forefront of your mind, you will develop a more purpose-driven strategy to achieving your goals, which will lead to greater motivation from yourself and staff.

Tip 2: Broaden your horizons

Envision the 'Big Picture' to unlock your motivation. Consider the broader implications of your goals, both personally and professionally. The ripple effect of your actions touches many lives, including family and colleagues. It can also help improve your community, inspire others and positively influence people you might never meet. Using this whole perspective helps you tap into all of your potential impact and leaves you inspired with a deeper feeling of motivation.

To keep motivated in your personal life, focus on creating deep and lasting relationships with family and friends. Also find projects that have a wider purpose than just you or family. You will find yourself motivated by engaging in your community, volunteering, or supporting projects that contribute to others' wellbeing.

In business, to increase motivation, create meaningful products that inspire and service customers' genuine needs, fostering loyalty and sustainable growth. Cultivate a purpose-driven culture within your business which values employee wellbeing, personal growth and collaboration. Generate profits, but also make a contribution back (community, charity, wherever) and involve your staff in deciding where it goes. This all plays a part in keeping your teams motivated.

Tip 3: Reverse the perspective

The cost of inaction is a powerful way to boost your motivation by considering the consequences of not achieving your goals. Reflect on how the lives of your family, your employees, your customers and your community would be different if you did not pursue your goals and dreams.

During one of the most challenging periods of my life, when I was fighting for my life during a six-week coma, this perspective became incredibly powerful. In those darkest moments, I had more to give. My death would affect not only family and friends, but also customers, staff and society as a whole.

This realisation helped give me the strength to fight for my life with total motivation. Embracing this perspective can help you understand the full importance of your goals and the true value of your dreams. By considering the total cost of inaction, you will discover deeper motivation to persevere, even in the face of adversity.

THINK BIG to tap into motivation; your actions have the power to transform lives, both personally and professionally, and by harnessing that power, you can achieve remarkable success and create a legacy that will inspire generations to come.

Nick Griffith Following a Masters in Engineering from Imperial College and working for Accenture, Nick founded The Digital Marketing Partnership agency.

Nick specialises in increasing conversions, traffic and engagement. He has helped many clients boost engagement and conversions over 200% using scorecards. He is also an expert in LinkedIn lead generation and automated follow-up funnels.

He is a problem-solver who has faced real challenges, like recovering his memory after a six-week coma and using Joint Ventures to fill the O2 London with 7,500+ attendees in six weeks.

In 2023, Nick co-founded Imperial AI, a company to help businesses maximise growth and cost savings using AI-powered tools.

🌐 www.digitalmarketingpartnership.com

🌐 www.imperialai.ai

in www.linkedin.com/in/nickrgriffith

Powerful Motivation Starts In The Heart

KEITH HOLDT

What is motivation, that driving force that compels individuals to act or behave in a certain way to achieve a desired goal or outcome?

Most have us have dreams, aims, goals and desires that we want to achieve, and the stronger the motivation – that energy that drives us to get out of our beds in the morning, willing to take on the odds and overcome sometimes insurmountable obstacles – the more likely we are to achieve our goals.

Motivation can be influenced by a wide range of factors, including internal factors such as personal values, interests and beliefs, as well as external factors such as rewards, recognition and feedback from others. But it can also be affected by emotions (positive and negative), desires and preferences.

Recently I was having a coffee with the CEO of a large, nationwide social enterprise. Over the thirty-plus years of their existence they have helped thousands of homeless people get back on their feet and have branched out into other activities in support of those less able.

Listening to him tell the story, I was inspired by the impact they had had. But he went on to share that he was concerned. It felt to him that post-Covid there was less energy in the business. The challenges of Covid had been embraced with a lot of energy – they had more than survived, and had been able to continue supporting those in need – but now it was beginning to feel lethargic. He didn't know what to do, but he knew he needed to find the missing spark urgently. They seemed to have lost their heart, that emotional driving force that had kept them going from strength to strength over so many years.

Having worked with hundreds of business leaders over many years, and even in looking at myself, I believe one of the strongest motivational forces we have is emotional and starts in the heart.

I have often asked these leaders what their main motivation was for the sacrifices they had made in building their businesses. Many times, the answer came down to money, or some other external ambition, but many of them were unhappy, and digging deeper into their businesses, I found that often their staff were equally unhappy. They were doing their day jobs to put food on the table, but were not really energised, not really looking forward to each day with the zest and zeal that would really bring about major success to the business, not fully committed to the business.

I have also observed something quite different in many of the businesses that have achieved stellar success. Energised, enthusiastic, motivated staff, often led by an energised, enthusiastic, motivated leader. What's the difference?

I define 'heart-led motivation' as motivation that comes from within and translates into actions that power and energise a person to achieve incredible outcomes. Leaders powered from within, from their emotions, are leaders that inspire their staff, their customers, their business partners, their 'people', to follow them. Think Steve Jobs, Martin Luther King, Nelson Mandela.

This is motivation that focuses on connecting with one's inner values, passions and purpose. It involves aligning one's actions and goals with what truly matters on a deep, emotional level, rather than just pursuing external rewards or societal expectations.

Heart-led motivation involves listening to one's intuition and inner guidance, and striving to create a meaningful and fulfilling life that is in alignment with one's core values and beliefs. It involves focusing on intrinsic motivation such as personal growth and self-improvement and contributing to a greater good rather than just seeking external validation or material rewards.

This approach to motivation can be particularly beneficial in the workplace, as it can lead to higher levels of engagement, productivity and satisfaction among employees who feel connected to their work and aligned with the company's mission and values. It can also foster a sense of purpose and fulfilment, both individually and collectively, leading to a positive impact on overall wellbeing and organisational success.

How, then, does heart-led motivation translate to the heart-led leader? This is a leader who focuses on leading with compassion, empathy and emotional intelligence. They put the needs and wellbeing of employees and stakeholders at the forefront, prioritising their personal and professional growth.

Heart-led leaders are committed to creating a positive work environment that fosters trust, collaboration and mutual respect. They encourage open communication and actively listen to their team members' ideas and feedback, valuing diverse perspectives and encouraging creativity and innovation.

These leaders lead by example and demonstrate a genuine concern for the welfare of their team members, customers and society. They prioritise ethical and sustainable practices and strive to make a positive impact on the world.

Overall, heart-led leadership is a people-centred approach that recognises the importance of emotional intelligence, empathy and compassion in creating a successful and fulfilling work environment – one in which their staff are equally motivated from the heart in their own day-to-day activities.

CASE STUDY: DEDICATION

Why is heart-led motivation and leadership so important to me? Most of us have had people in our lives who were a major influence on us. In my case, it was my grandfather, Keith Gordon Leonard, who has been my lifelong inspiration. A highly intelligent and stern man who didn't speak much and suffered fools less, but who was led from his heart and inspired those around him.

I was six years old when he decided it was time to show me around his business, one of South Africa's largest manufacturers and suppliers of furnaces to the gold mining industry. He had started from his garage, welding gates and fences. The business grew, adapted and evolved until it became the big engineering company that he showed the six-year-old me.

I remember the day clearly. The images are still strong in my memory. He showed me his office, with its large wooden desk, then took me around the factory where different furnaces were at different stages of completion. He introduced me to his foreman, then the rest of the staff. I watched as they welded the steel. I held my ears as the sparks flew as they cut through metal. I walked by his side holding his hand with a feeling of awe and complete pride that my grandad had built this, as he explained the important and significant parts of it as simply as he could so that this six-year-old could understand. As I looked up at the high ceilings of the factory, standing mesmerised by the sparks, the hammering, and the noise, I was filled with awe and inspiration. One question kept going through my mind. 'How did he build this business? What was the secret?'

There are many lessons I learned from my grandfather, but my strongest memory was of his passion, dedication, love for the business and the people who worked for him, matched by the passion, dedication, respect and love his people had for him, all equally committed to the task at hand.

I went on to study the engineering degree my grandfather never did. I studied how to optimise processes, how to design shop floors, how to manage inventory. With the law students I studied basic commercial law, with the accounting students the fundamentals of finance, with the MBA students the science of management. All the time driven by my desire to understand how it all clicked together. I've worked as an engineer, management consultant, global sales executive, investor and entrepreneur across many different industries. I have advised and worked with many different business leaders and businesses through their frequent ups and downs. And I have seen first-hand that those who have weathered the storms, and achieved meaningful success, have often been those with leaders who have been motivated from the heart, giving them the energy to lead from the front, no matter what the odds and filling their people with energy and enthusiasm to deliver the required results.

Top Tips

Here are some top tips for heart-led motivation:

1. **Identify your values and purpose:** Spend time reflecting on what really matters to you and what you want to achieve. Clarify your values and goals, and make sure that your work or activities align with them. Is what is driving you internal or external?

2. **Focus on the positive:** Rather than dwelling on the negative aspects of your work or situation, focus on the positive. Look for opportunities to grow, learn and make a positive impact.

3. **Practise self-care:** Take care of your physical, emotional and mental health. Make time for activities that bring you joy and relaxation, such as exercise, meditation or spending time in nature.

4. **Cultivate supportive relationships:**
   Surround yourself with people who support and
   encourage you. Seek out mentors or role models
   who inspire you and can offer guidance and
   support.

5. **Celebrate your successes:** Recognise and
   celebrate your accomplishments, no matter how
   small they may seem. Take time to acknowledge
   your hard work and progress and use this as
   motivation to continue pushing yourself.

6. **Embrace challenges:** Rather than avoiding
   challenges or difficult tasks, embrace them as
   opportunities to grow and learn. Approach them
   with a positive mindset and a willingness to learn
   from mistakes.

7. **Show compassion and empathy in
   leadership:** Towards your family, your staff,
   your customers and your business partners. Are
   you inspiring, energising and motivating them, or
   taking the oxygen out of the air?

8. **Stay true to your heart:** Finally, stay true to
   your heart and your values, even when faced
   with obstacles or difficult decisions. Trust your
   intuition and be willing to take risks in pursuit of
   your goals and dreams.

David Mitchell, head teacher at Dunoon Grammar School, a state school in the small Scottish town of Dunoon, is one of the most passionate and driven leaders I have met. The buzz and energy hits you as you walk through the door, happy teachers and students, with signs of the school's achievements dotted around the hallways of the school. David is always positive, and always focused on the next thing for the school to achieve, motivated by his love for the students and his passion for preparing them for successful lives ahead. In 2022, he led the school to winning the prestigious Global Community Collaboration Award. In 2023, he was shortlisted as Scottish Head Teacher of the year, putting him on course to being put forward as Head Teacher of the year across the United Kingdom. On each occasion I meet with him, I leave feeling energised and uplifted. A true leader, leading from the heart, both for himself and for those surrounding him. Inspirational and uplifting. Heart-led motivation and leadership powerfully in action.

If only there were more like him. There could be. It could be you.

Keith Holdt is an expert at helping businesses achieve results they didn't think were possible through ways they didn't know were there.

Over the course of an international career, he has been on every side of the table and has helped businesses deliver over £1 billion of shareholder returns. This experience has provided him with invaluable insight and understanding into what makes a successful business leader.

Based on his many experiences, he has authored the booklet *You are the Captain of your Ship*, aimed at helping both businesses and individuals cultivate the right mindset, focus, pace and discipline to achieving their goals, which has received wide acclaim for its simplicity and clarity.

Motivation Is Chasing An Orange Ball

JOHN LUNN

It's early spring 2023, the trees are starting to come out of their sleep and the days are finally getting longer. I am out in the early dawn walking Whisky, our cocker spaniel, in Kensington Gardens with the rumbling noise in the background as the city starts to wake up. The park is quiet, and we stop to play games; Whisky's favourite is fetching an orange ball from as far as possible. He chases it down and brings it back every time, getting a treat in return. The joy in his eyes and face is infectious. There is no doubt that Whisky is highly motivated to please.

In the corner of my eye, I see the unmistakably tall figure of Nick Cave, the singer and actor, walking towards us across the grass as he heads towards Hyde Park. As he passes by, he smiles and remarks on what a happy dog Whisky seems to be and how motivated he is to keep bringing the ball back. I thank him, replying that the orange ball is the motivation, not the owner. We laugh and go our separate ways.

Motivation is derived from the Latin word *movere*, which means 'to move'. Psychologists describe motivation as the internal and external forces that drive us to achieve an outcome. While Whisky's world of chasing orange balls is straightforward, as I look back on motivation in my life and the friends and people I have met over the years, I reflect on how motivation can drive extraordinary outcomes in business and personal lives.

CASE STUDY: FINDING PURPOSE

In the Netflix *Chef's Table*[3] series, some of the world's top chefs share their stories of how they were motivated to create extraordinary businesses. In episode 13, the focus is Alain Passard, the owner of the three Michelin-star restaurant L'Arpège in Paris.

The documentary profiles the beautiful restaurant, the team and Alain's career. The story's core is Alain's decision in 2001 to completely change the restaurant's focus

---

3   Netflix, 'Chef's Table: France, Alain Passard', Netflix (2 September 2016)

away from traditional French cuisine to become a wholly vegetarian restaurant.

His motivation was deciding that the restaurant needed to change focus, and he was determined to make it happen. The Michelin team said he was foolish, his three stars would be removed, and that a vegetarian restaurant would not succeed in a meat-obsessed France. He ignored their advice, closed the restaurant and reopened with vegetables at the 'centre of the plate'.

A year later, the Michelin team returned, tasted the food – and gave him three stars. I have been fortunate to meet Alain and eat at his restaurant. The food is exceptional. What is most inspiring is the story behind his restaurant and the clarity of purpose that drove him to risk everything and create something he wanted.

In my life, I have been lucky to have worked in many businesses and great teams. There have been many highs and some lows; one of the highlights was growing, building and selling a change management consulting firm, Moorhouse.

Management consulting is dominated by large accounting and consulting firms like EY, KPMG, PwC and Deloitte, cumulatively generating over $150 billion in fees in 2022. The challenge with Moorhouse was to create a boutique alternative to these firms, attracting highly motivated talent into the firm and creating something extraordinary in providing services to clients.

Like the David and Goliath fable, competing head-to-head with these large firms to win clients and attract talent was a huge challenge with the assets at their disposal. We had to think differently to have any chance of competing in this market. As a collective leadership team, we believed there was an opportunity to build a disruptor in the industry by creating a highly motivated, purpose-led business and a high-performing leadership capability at the organisation's heart.

The very start of the journey was discussions and conversations from across the team on what our WHY was, as articulated brilliantly by Simon Sinek[4] in his books and TED Talks. This led to various discussions, debates and thinking about what we could realistically achieve – from the revenue targets, service offerings, business size and clients we would target. Some voices challenged what could be achieved and wanted the business to remain as it was – sometimes leading to them leaving the organisation. While this was disruptive, we defined a set of principles agreed across the organisation which became the foundation for the organisation's future success. This was distilled in a 1:3:5 framework which described the WHAT, WHYs and HOWs for our future, together with our 'Flag' which visually articulated the future business.

The results were exceptional. Over seven years we quadrupled revenues and profit together as a team. We

---

4   S Sinek, et al, *Find Your WHY, a practical guide for discovering purpose for your team* (2017, Penguin Random House)

partnered with some of the most prominent organisations across the FTSE100 and public sector, including Goldman Sachs, GSK, NHS and the Bank of England, on some of their most challenging and complex change programmes. We competed and won engagements against the big four consulting firms and built a reputation for providing highly motivated teams delivering exceptional results.

CASE STUDY: INNER WORK LIFE

There is helpful academic research that supports the evidence of how a purpose-led organisation drives business performance. Theresa Amabile, a professor at Harvard, has looked at the question of what makes people happy and motivated at work with her colleague Steve Kramer. They identified three primary sources of motivation:

1. Extrinsic: Working for money or other benefits and rewards.

2. Intrinsic: Doing work for the love of it.

3. Altruistic: Doing the work to connect with, and provide value to, others.

Their 'Intrinsic Motivation Principle of Creativity'[5] identified that people are most creative when motivated by doing work that makes them feel interested, curious, satisfied and challenged.

---

5   T Amabile, *Componential Theory of Creativity*, Harvard Business School (26 April 2012), www.hbs.edu/ris/Publication%20Files/12-096. pdf, accessed 29 June 2023

The 'Inner Work Life' principle identifies the elements that drive improved performance – the most substantial level of intrinsic motivation about the world, positive feelings about the team and those people you're working with, and being positive and proud about themselves.

In their research, the most critical event that improved motivation was making progress on an activity, something that is meaningful. This is critical to creating work engagement, which drives the bottom line.

We are more likely to be enthusiastic about work when it aligns with our WHY as opposed to 'because we must'.

CASE STUDY: RECOGNISE YOUR GOALS TO CREATE RESULTS

In the early days of Moorhouse, we defined our WHAT, WHYs and HOWs and started to create a motivated team. Commercial success was yet to come, and our journey took the inevitable twists and turns as we went forward.

To help build our environment and align motivations across the team, we took inspiration from the story of the Great Britain men's rowing eight team that entered the Sydney 2000 Olympics. Distilled into the book *Will It Make Ghe Boat Go Faster?*[6] the Olympian Ben Hunt-Davies, together with executive coach Harriet Beveridge, describe previous failed attempts to win Olympic Gold and the change of environment established for the 2000 Olympics.

---

6   H Beveridge and B Hunt-Davies, *Will It Make The Boat Go Faster? Olympic-winning strategies for everyday success* (Matador, 2011)

Recognising that the team had to operate differently to achieve its goal, they outline focusing on goals and motivation, filtering out unhelpful information, dealing with change and overcoming setbacks.

In keeping the team motivated, a simple question was asked when faced with choices: 'Will it make the boat go faster?' If not, a different choice would be made. This helped focus on the environment to get results, rather than the results alone, and the importance of building in continuous feedback. The team won the gold medal, beating the favourites, Australia, by less than a second.

Right from the start, we adopted this approach. We knew the results we sought over the long term (in effect, our 'Olympic Gold'), so we asked ourselves as a business throughout the process, 'Will it make the boat go faster?'

CASE STUDY: THE BENEFITS OF CONNECTING WITH NATURE

Following the sale and exit of the business, I had the opportunity to take some time out and be part of a completely different environment.

I chose to study gardening at the Chelsea Physic Garden in London, one of the world's earliest botanic gardens, established in 1673. I also joined the Society of Garden Designers (SGD). One of the first events I attended was the SGD's Annual Conference held in London at the Royal Geographical Society. I was struck by the high level of energy, motivation and purpose within the conference room.

In her book *A Well-Gardened Mind: The Restorative Power of Nature*,[7] the psychiatrist Sue Stuart-Smith outlines her thesis that gardening and connecting with nature provides a wide range of benefits for mental health. She provides perspectives, having worked with clients on how environments can provide a sense of achievement and purpose, reduce stress and anxiety and improve mood and self-esteem.

Also in the UK, Isabella Tree provides a fascinating insight in her book, *The Book of Wilding: A practical guide to rewilding, big and small*,[8] into how she transformed the family farm from traditional farming to a rewilding approach. The concept of rewilding is to create conditions for wildlife to thrive, re-establishing natural processes to repair ecosystems and boost biodiversity. Organisations are on a similar journey of creating new operating models, closer collaborations with their supply chains and improving social conditions.

Finally, across the other side of the world in South Africa, Boyd Varty is known for his work in the African bushveld, motivated by his connection with nature and the harmonious relationship between humans and the natural world. In his book *The Lion Tracker's Guide to Life*,[9] he parallels tracking in the bush with how we live our lives and understanding our gifts, purpose and mission. He provides a beautiful quote as the motto of a tracker, 'I

---

7   S Stuart-Smith, *A Well-Gardened Mind: The Restorative Power of Nature* (William Collins, April 2020)

8   I Tree, *The Book of Wilding: A practical guide to rewilding, big and small* (Bloomsbury Publishing, 2023)

9   B Varty, *The Lion Tracker's Guide to Life* (Houghton Mifflin Harcourt, 2019)

don't know where we are going, but I know exactly how to get there.'

These connections with nature and the opportunity to build new ecosystems in our organisations with a clarity of purpose and social responsibility are our opportunity to track a new way forward.

Top Tips

1. **Build purpose at the heart of your organisation:** Build a clear Purpose on Why the organisation or team exists, supported by Values (How), Mission (What) and Vision (Where). Incorporate the United Nations Sustainable Development Goals[10] into the Purpose to focus on the opportunity to become a sustainable business. Make it meaningful.

2. **Communicate an inspiring vision:** Focus on making the boat go faster. Leverage the opportunity in the accelerated shift in mindsets to create sustainable businesses and set a vision which is inspiring and motivating. Connect work with the vision, demonstrate commitment.

3. **Foster curiosity:** Encourage teams to explore new ideas, experiment and ask questions to seek

---

10 United Nations, 'The 17 Goals' (2015), https://sdgs.un.org/goals, accessed 21 July 2023

new innovative solutions to today's challenges, building on the intrinsic motivation principle of creativity.

This is your call to action. Help to create tomorrow's businesses today.

John Lunn supports teams to deliver strategy, business transformation and growth. Previously CEO of the B Corp Reset, he was also a board member at Moorhouse and a partner at PA Consulting Group. John focuses on building purpose-driven, future-focused, sustainable businesses. He is also an award-winning garden designer, beekeeper, producer of Lunny Honey and co-owner of a working cocker spaniel, Whisky.

🌐 www.reimaginednow.com

in www.LinkedIn.com/in/strategyintoaction

◻ www.instagram.com/thejohnlunn

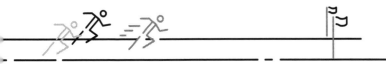

Motivation Is Having A Goal...

GARETH MARTINDALE

Motivation is having a goal... OK, I get it, sounds too simple, right? But when you have a clear goal, you magnetise yourself to it. This means the methods will materialise. As the compass needle finds its way to the magnetic north, your inner motivation compass will direct you to your goal. You just need to know what your magnetic north is, and the journey will unfold before you.

To me, motivation is the fuel that propels you forwards, the driving force that keeps you going even when the going gets tough. It's the burning desire to achieve something, the relentless pursuit of personal and professional growth. As a creative design agency owner, I've come to realise that motivation is not just about reaching my goals, but also about aiding my clients in discovering and accomplishing theirs.

Success hinges on having clearly defined goals that are measurable and time-bound. The clearer your goals, the easier it becomes to devise a plan of action and take steps towards achieving them. They draw people, ideas and resources towards you. The clearer the goal, the more potent the magnet.

I firmly believe that everyone has a unique source of motivation, a wellspring of energy within them that can be tapped into to yield powerful results. This inner drive is what pushes people to strive for improvement, surmount obstacles and, ultimately, achieve the goals they have set for themselves.

CASE STUDY: CREATIVITY

My own journey began when I discovered my passion for design and branding. I was twelve years old. Art had always been my favourite subject, but on one occasion, my usual Art teacher took a leave of absence and was temporarily replaced by a substitute teacher. He was a 'Graphic Designer', a term I had never heard of before. He arrived carrying a large A1-sized portfolio packed with sketches, logo designs and other magical creations. I had never considered the idea that things were 'designed' with intention, that a logo had been meticulously crafted with such attention to detail, or that immense consideration had been devoted to aspects like typography, colour and shape. I came to understand that each element of design was deliberately chosen to convey specific messages and evoke particular emotions, all working in harmony to create a coherent and captivating brand identity. Up until that point, I had always regarded art as a hobby, something I would enjoy in my spare time alongside a 'proper job'. We spent the entire lesson delving into his sketchbooks and listening intently to the story of his own journey. That day, I discovered my 'magnetic north'.

Throughout my journey, I was captivated by the idea of creating unique identities for businesses, helping them stand out in a crowded marketplace. But to be successful, I needed to understand not just the mechanics of branding, but also the psychology behind it – how people think, feel and respond to various stimuli. And that's where my fascination with motivation came in.

For my clients, motivation is equally important. I always begin by helping them define their goals, identify their target audience and craft a compelling brand story. I've come to understand that motivation is a critical element in crafting successful branding strategies. By understanding what drives their customers, we can create campaigns that resonate deeply and inspire action.

Penny Power OBE, Founder of Business is Personal and client of Sherbert Lemon, says:

'As a business owner, my brand and how I come across is important. This was especially important when I was creating visuals that I could use in talks and online when I was launching my new book, *Business Is Personal*.

'I am very impact driven, however, sometimes we just lose motivation as tasks overtake the joy of staying in the "purpose" zone, and one of the tasks I had on my list pre-publication was to create some branding assets that would display throughout the book. The joy I felt when they were sent to me by Gareth was deep. Suddenly my message was in a graphic, and it made such sense to me when I saw them. I had many business benefits from having a clear brand around my message, however, the unexpected aspect of the graphics was the way this motivated me. Having these assets at hand for me to use liberated me. I could design slides and write social media posts, always sharing the images and sharing what they stood for. I now see that graphic images set you free. Without the branding and imagery, you are dull – not only to your potential clients, but also to yourself.

'It is so easy now to use online tools to mock up something that is "good enough", however, it is the skill in the interpretation by someone with that expertise, that person who can see what you are saying, that's important. Transforming words into images. To me, it is the starting point of a project, product or company. Imagery is the building block. It provides motivation to be known by more people from those moments, so in my opinion, investing in graphics is the foundation of any new idea.'

This quote from Penny highlights the profound impact a clear, well-developed brand can have on someone's motivation. The importance of a brand in shaping an individual's self-perception, especially as a business owner, cannot be understated. It's a tangible representation of one's identity, values and vision, playing a critical role in creating connections with audiences and establishing a unique position in the market.

Over the years, I've developed certain habits to keep my motivation levels high. For instance, I start each day by reviewing my goals and visualising the steps I need to take to achieve them. This mental exercise helps me maintain a clear sense of direction and sets the tone for the day.

Another habit I've cultivated is celebrating small victories. Whether it's a client's positive feedback, a new project win or the completion of a challenging task, I make it a point to acknowledge and celebrate these milestones. This not only keeps me motivated, but also helps build a positive mindset that spills over into my work with clients. A little pat on the back goes a long way.

As my experience and expertise grew, I found myself becoming a mentor and guide to others in the branding industry. Through workshops, webinars and one-on-one consultations, I've had the opportunity to share my knowledge and insights with countless individuals eager to learn about branding and motivation. This, in turn, has allowed me to refine my own understanding of motivation and how it can be harnessed to create powerful results for clients.

One key lesson I've learned through my work is the importance of adaptability. Motivation isn't a one-size-fits-all phenomenon; it can take different forms for different people. It's my job to understand my clients' unique motivational drivers and tailor my approach accordingly. Sometimes this means tapping into their sense of ambition and competition, while at other times it may involve appealing to their desire for connection and community. By staying flexible and empathetic, I'm able to create branding strategies that truly resonate with my clients and their target audiences.

I know this next part is easier said than done, especially for an entrepreneur, but the value of maintaining a healthy work-life balance is *hugely* important. It can be easy to become consumed by professional goals and ambitions, but I've found that taking the time to recharge and nurture my personal interests and relationships has a significant impact on my overall motivation and wellbeing. By prioritising self-care and maintaining a balanced lifestyle,

I'm able to bring more energy, creativity and enthusiasm to my work with clients.

In essence, my journey has been a continuous process of learning, growing and evolving, with motivation as my creative companion. By understanding the power of motivation and how it can be harnessed in service to our goals, I've been able to navigate the complex world of branding with confidence, resilience and a healthy dose of playfulness (my favourite bit).

Top Tips

Over time I've discovered a few key tips that have helped me stay motivated, and I believe they can work for you too:

1. **Define your goals clearly:** Clarity is the first step towards motivation. When you know exactly what you're working towards, it's easier to stay focused and maintain momentum. Take the time to write down your goals, both personal and professional, and be specific about what you want to achieve. This will act as your roadmap, guiding you towards your desired destination.

2. **Embrace the power of visualisation:** Your imagination is a powerful tool for motivation. By visualising the successful completion of your goals, you're creating a mental image that can

propel you forwards. Spend a few minutes each day picturing yourself achieving your objectives, feeling the emotions associated with success and experiencing the rewards that come with accomplishment. This practice can help to solidify your commitment to your goals and increase your drive to achieve them.

3. **Surround yourself with positivity:** Your environment plays a significant role in your motivation levels. Make it a point to surround yourself with positive influences – people who inspire and uplift you, activities that energise and rejuvenate you and resources that educate and empower you. By immersing yourself in a supportive and encouraging atmosphere, you'll be more likely to stay motivated and maintain the momentum needed to reach your goals.

4. **Don't be hard on yourself:** This is crucial for your mental health and wellbeing. We all have good days and not so good days. We can't be motivated 100% of the time. Sometimes we need to take a step back and relax, recharge and refocus. If you're not 'in the zone', that's OK. Allow yourself this time, it's what your body and mind need. It doesn't mean you've lost your spark, it's all part of your journey.

Motivation is the magnetic force that draws us towards our goals and helps us overcome the challenges that inevitably arise along the way. I've learned that understanding and harnessing motivation is crucial not only for my own success, but also for the success of those around us and the people who mean the most to us. By defining clear goals, embracing the power of visualisation and surrounding ourselves with positivity, we can tap into our inner drive and achieve remarkable results in our personal and professional lives. So go ahead, discover your magnetic north and let motivation be your guide on this incredible journey.

Gareth Martindale is a seasoned Graphic Designer, Brand Consultant and Creative Design Agency owner with a passion for helping businesses create compelling visual identities. With a rich background working in top-tier agencies, Gareth went on to share his knowledge and expertise as a university lecturer, shaping the next generation of creative professionals. Today, as the founder and owner of the successful Creative Design Agency, Sherbert Lemon, Gareth oversees offices in both the UK and Dubai, delivering exceptional branding solutions for a diverse clientele across the globe. His unique blend of creativity, experience and motivational insight has established him as a highly sought-after authority in the world of branding and design.

🌐 https://sherbertlemon.co.uk

in www.linkedin.com/in/garethmartindale

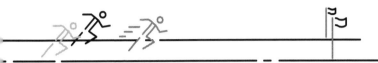

True Motivation Comes From Inspiration

OWEN O'MALLEY

When you are inspired to achieve a goal, motivation will only get you so far. Sustained motivation requires inspiration to keep you going long term. Motivation is like being in a hot bath: eventually, you get out of the bath and do something. Some say commitment is to do the task long after the initial motivation to do the task has left you.

My definition of commitment is that you either achieve your goal, or you die while in the process of achieving your goal. Words have power; when you listen to someone who says they are committed to doing a task, this carries more weight than when they say they are motivated to do a task.

Motivation can be temporary and inspiration can be more profound; however, commitment is where the true power to get tasks completed is to be found. Somebody who is motivated to lose weight and interested in jogging might easily be deterred by a rainy day. A committed person will put on some rainproof clothes and go for a run regardless of the weather.

To be fully committed to completing a task, your rational brain must outwit your irrational brain. 'What does this mean?' you may say. Well, it requires a deeper understanding of the relationship between our conscious and subconscious minds.

Einstein espoused that one of the most important attributes you and I have as human beings is the power to imagine that which is not yet made manifest. The subconscious mind is programmed to precisely follow the exact instructions that the conscious mind thinks about. When realised, this is a very powerful formula to help you succeed and achieve your dreams and goals. If you think you are going to be successful, the subconscious mind must obey your command like the genie in *Aladdin*.

It is important that we stand guard at the door between our conscious and subconscious mind. We must be highly selective about what thoughts we let slip past from our conscious mind into our subconscious programmer, which is the one that produces the results in our life.

If you follow some of the Dr Joe Dispenza research,[11] he digs deeper into this concept. Dr Dispenza talks about how you must pull your mind out of your body. He has proven scientifically that our thoughts become so much a part of who we are that at a cellular and genomic level we become what we think about. Hence, our thoughts define us and are responsible for our subconscious patterns, which, in turn, determine the results in our life.

It is said that we have, on average, 60,000 thoughts per day, which is impressive. What is less impressive is that 90% of those thoughts are repeated every day.[12] This does not leave much room for the process of imagining new thoughts and creating new and better outcomes in our life.

CASE STUDY: SUCCESS MEANS STARTING YOUNG

On 11 March 1942, as World War II was raging in Europe, a young boy, aged eleven, had dreamed of becoming the richest man in the world. He had saved up some money from working a paper delivery job and invested his total savings of $114.75 to buy three shares of Cities Services, a

---

11   Unlimited Dr Joe Dispenza, www.drjoedispenza.com, accessed 21 July 2023

12   C Comaford, 'Got Inner Peace? 5 Ways To Get It NOW', *Forbes* (4 April 2012), www.forbes.com/sites/christinecomaford/2012/04/04/got-inner-peace-5-ways-to-get-it-now, accessed 21 July 2023

company trading in the stock market. That man is Warren Buffett. He has achieved the status of richest man in the world many times. He is currently worth over $100 billion dollars.[13]

To put into perspective the achievement of accumulating even one of his $100 billion dollars, consider this: if I were to transfer one dollar per second into your bank account, it would take me twelve days to deposit one million dollars into your account, but thirty-two years to transfer one billion into your account. It would, therefore, take me 320 years, at the rate of one dollar per second, to transfer to your account what Warren Buffett has achieved in just over eighty years.

Let us examine how Warren achieved such greatness, what his key influencers were and whose success he modelled. First of all, his father was a stockbroker who served four terms as a congressman and encouraged Warren to pursue his studies despite Warren's desire to stop his education after high school and become an entrepreneur.

Warren was inspired by a library book he read at age seven called *One Thousand Ways to Make $1000*.[14] He worked at his grandfather's grocery store, as well as selling chewing gum, Coca-Cola and weekly magazines door-to door.

At age ten, Warren's father took him to visit the New York Stock Exchange, an event that was to shape his life for

---

13   J Wolinsky, 'What is Warren Buffett's net wealth?', MoneyWeek (last updated 16 June 2023), https://moneyweek.com/economy/entrepreneurs/605940/warren-buffett-net-wealth

14   P Fox, *One Thousand Ways to Make $1000* (Stanford Publishing, 2019)

decades to come. Warren also made money from delivering newspapers, selling golf balls and stamps. Later on, he progressed to buying and placing pinball machines in the local barbers' shops. He earned his first passive income from these pinball machines.

Ironically rejected by Harvard Business School, Warren chose to study at Columbia University when he discovered that Benjamin Graham, the famous author of the 'bible of investing' called *The Intelligent Investor* was a lecturer there.[15] These were the most valuable lessons that Warren learned from Ben about investing, which he later described as: 'The basic ideas of investing are to look at stocks as business, use the market's fluctuations to your advantage and seek a margin of safety. That is what Ben Graham taught us. A hundred years from now they will still be the cornerstones of investing.'[16]

One of Warren's most successful partnerships and the man that has influenced him the most is Charlie Munger, who Warren has worked with since 1959. At age ninety-nine, today Charlie is an inspiration to Warren who has many times expressed gratitude for their long-lasting friendship and partnership.

They have successfully steered their Berkshire Hathaway fund since 1965 and despite having only a handful of people show up at the first AGM, they both had a vision of thousands of people at future AGMs. Sure enough, over

15   B Graham, *The Intelligent Investor* (Harper Business, October 2003)

16   Outlook Money, 'Be greedy when others are fearful: Warren Buffett's Top Five Investing Lessons', Outlook (31 August 2022), www.outlookindia.com/business/be-greedy-when-others-are-fearful-warren-buffett-s-top-five-investing-lessons-news-220197, accessed 10 August 2023

50,000 investors travelled from all over the world to attend their 50th anniversary AGM in 2015.[17]

17 M Udland, 'This is what it's like to be a shareholder at Berkshire Hathaway's annual meeting', Insider (3 May 2015), www.businessinsider.com/berkshire-hathaway-annual-meeting-2015-2015-5?r=US&IR=T, accessed 21 July 2023

I, and many of my team leaders, have been blessed to attend many of Warren Buffett's and Charlie Munger's Berkshire Hathaway AGMs over the past two decades and would highly recommend witnessing their wisdom and being inspired by their greatness.

Top Tips

Environment is critical to our success in that we become the average of the people we hang out with. The concept that you will only earn the average of the five people that you spend most time with can be a motivation to find wealthier people to hang out with and learn from. That is the power of books and videos now that we did not have in the past – we can now 'hang out' with the wealthiest people on the planet through the power of YouTube, Spotify, etc. We are on the verge, as a species, of finding out what the power of AI and science will do for our development and capabilities in the future.

Accelerated learning, together with application, is the key to success in the modern age. 'Knowledge is power' is a popular phrase, but true power is found in the application of the knowledge. 'Do the thing and you shall have the power' is another powerful quotation from George Zalucki's talk called *The Profile of a Champion*.[18]

One of the most powerful ways to learn is to read and listen to the same words at the same time while in an alpha brainwave state of mind. Having classical music playing quietly in the background while you study can be a powerful tool to avoid distractions.

One of the key ingredients to motivation is to find out what you are truly passionate about and make it your mission in life to pursue your passion. Some say if you do not know what your passion is, make it your mission in life to find out your true purpose and passion.

Vision is another critical cornerstone to motivation. Create a future vision of yourself and allow your life to be all about fulfilling that future vision of yourself. All great achievers talk about seeing the victory or the goal way before it happened. They talk about how the rational mind does not know the difference between that which is imagined and that which is real.

Some ancient texts talk about how you must let your rational mind outwit your irrational mind, meaning that if your subconscious mind does not know what is real and

---

18   George Zalucki, Original MP3 version of Profile Of A Champion, https://georgezalucki.com/product/original-profile-of-a-champion, accessed 21 July 2023

what is imagined, you can direct your subconscious mind to create the future before it has happened. With that unwavering vision of your future self being ever present, the subconscious mind, always plugged into the universal consciousness, will deliver people, places and things that will make manifest your vision and your dreams.

If you think that this is somewhat far-fetched, know that you are already creating your future with your thoughts. If you are unaware of saying non-supporting things to yourself like: 'Why does this bad thing always happen to me?', you are sending an embedded command to your subconscious mind that constantly reinforces the pattern of that bad thing always happening to you now and in the future.

You must stand guard to the door of your precious mind. Only think supporting thoughts and be very conscious of every word you say, every thought you think, every action you take and every deed you do. Some spiritual teachers would say that everything, and I mean everything, is sacred in that every thought, deed, word and action affects the next seven generations of your family and your legacy.

Your task now is to find your purpose and your passion, create a future vision of yourself, imagine that the future has already happened and happily live your life. With this strategy in place, you will never have a challenge with being motivated ever again. People will be in awe of your power, purpose and clarity and they will rally around you to help you achieve your dreams as they become inspired by your vision of a better future for you and for them. As Martin Luther King said: 'I have a dream…'

Owen O'Malley is on a thirty-year mission to create one million millionaires using the powerful global stock market as a vehicle. He has initiated over 1,000 investment clubs in fifty-two different countries. He has educated over 25,000 people in fifteen different languages.

He has authored and co-authored ten books and has spoken at many large global events. He has been interviewed on national radio and television and has a built a powerful team of educators and traders, teaching people to make their money work harder.

Owen and his team have also empowered teenagers to understand how the global stock markets work. His purpose and passion are to bring financial literacy skills to this and future generations to come.

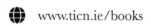 www.ticn.ie/books

Motivation Is Essential When Your Back Is Against The Wall

ALISON SHADRACK

Life doesn't always go to plan and nor do businesses. Motivation is an essential and everyday element in an entrepreneur's toolbox, but it's most critical when things aren't going to plan – so much so that your back's against the wall.

The recent pandemic wreaked havoc in many business sectors and, sadly, caused many businesses to close or reduce their workforce. Recessions and other events have long caused similar outcomes. While I don't believe you can necessarily 'motivate' your way out of everything, I do believe that it can help to make those outcomes better.

Many people may struggle to magic motivation out of thin air when they are feeling despondent, at their lowest point, challenged by impossible obstacles or have little financial or other resources available to them.

But it's precisely during those low moments that motivation is critical and will play the most important part in securing a successful, or at least a more favourable, outcome. If you're not able to turn on the motivation at this point, when else would it serve you, your family, your team or your business better?

Telling someone to pick themselves up, pull themselves together or stop feeling sorry for themselves for their own sake, or even for their business or team's sake, is probably not super-helpful. The most powerful force of motivation comes from within.

I believe it's often when our backs are against the wall, when we face adversity or a sense of urgency, that motivation can surge to new heights and enable us to grow exponentially. For some, that may be growth in terms of personal development or leadership skills and for others it may relate to a positive turnaround in business revenue and growth.

But why does motivation become more accessible and potent in challenging circumstances? I believe understanding this phenomenon can help us harness the power of motivation in our everyday lives.

- **Fear of failure:** Have you ever had that sinking feeling when you have a looming deadline that you're struggling to meet? I know I have many a time, including writing this very chapter. The fear of failure is certainly a powerful motivator to get things done or started. The consequences of not taking action or falling short of expectations can be daunting. This fear ignites a sense of urgency and can push us to exert ourselves beyond our comfort zones. The pressure to succeed can awaken dormant motivation and drive us to push harder, persevere and strive for excellence.

- **Desire to prove oneself:** Adversity often brings out an inherent desire to prove that we are capable of achieving our goals, in spite of the challenge. We become even more motivated to demonstrate our abilities, competence and resilience. The sense of pride and accomplishment derived from rising above adversity can be a significant source of motivation.

- **Increased focus and clarity:** Challenging circumstances tend to eliminate distractions and create laser-like focus. When the pressure is on, we can find ourselves in a state of heightened concentration and clarity. The urgency of the situation forces us to prioritise our tasks, eliminate non-essential activities and dedicate our energy to what truly matters. This enhanced focus eliminates procrastination and propels us into action, bolstering our motivation.

- **Sense of purpose and meaning:** Difficult situations have a way of reminding us of our purpose and the importance of our business activities. When faced with a crisis, we are reminded of the significance of our goals and aspirations. This reminder instils a sense of purpose and meaning, acting as a fuel for motivation. The understanding that our actions can make a difference or lead to personal growth inspires us to persevere, regardless of the challenges we may encounter.

CASE STUDY: PLANTED NOT BURIED

Sometimes, when you're in a dark place, you tend to think you have been buried; but what if you've been planted?

Growing up, my dream was to be an Olympic athlete – I first started athletics when I was around six years old and followed my big sister into hurdling. From a very young age, I was disciplined into setting goals, working hard to achieve them, picking myself up (literally) off the ground every single time I fell over a hurdle, patching myself up (literally with plasters) and getting back on to the track to jump some more. By the age of seventeen, a number of difficult challenges, including injury and the pressure to become financially independent (ie, go and get a real job), led me to giving up on my first dream.

Although it was a challenging time, I had no concept at that point that everything I had learned and been through as a young athlete (resilience, tenacity, teamwork, discipline, etc) was going to stand me in such good stead in my adult life – both personally and in business.

It was my motivation and sheer determination to move out from my parents' home and become financially independent that led me to securing an incredible opportunity to work at the European Commission in Brussels, Belgium, in a marketing and events management role. I was nineteen, with a generous salary, housing and travel allowance. I set my goal of financial independence, but initially I had no clue what the job might be, where it might be or how the hell I was going to make it happen.

I knew it was up to me to make it happen. But by talking about my intention with others, doors started to open and people came forward to help me. It wasn't plain sailing and in fact the week before I was due to fly out to Brussels to start my new role (life), it all fell through as there was an issue with my age. I was too young! They offered me a job back near my home town, but I knew that would mean I would have to continue living at home (not my goal). So, I declined the offer and moved to Brussels anyway to look for a job and secured a temporary admin role within two weeks. It was an awful job or, more to the point, I think I was doing an awful job of it. But a few weeks in, I got a call from the director at the European Commission who had interviewed me previously as he had heard what I had done. He was so impressed with my tenacity that he said he had found a resolution to my age issue and asked me to start the following week in my marketing role.

I have to stress I didn't think I was doing anything special at the time – this was a game of survival for me. I will always be thankful to those who helped me along the way.

My friends back home thought I had lucked out, but in my eyes, they could have done the same thing – they just didn't have a goal or the motivation to pursue it.

Since that first experience of setting a goal and achieving it in 'real life', I have continued to achieve many more goals in my personal and professional life. Needless to say, I have fallen over many 'hurdles' along the way too.

In March 2020, my business Adia PR was six years old, we had a lovely office, great team, great clients and a nice micro-lifestyle business. But when Covid hit, we lost 50% of our clients in one week – phone call after phone call, clients were asking to 'pause' their contracts. Legally, I didn't have to agree to this request, but I knew that, somehow, we would be OK and get through whatever was coming.

My team was so supportive and the furlough scheme was a godsend. I talked with each team member to see who wanted to take advantage of the scheme and who preferred to stay and work. It was a 50-50 split. Within three months, I had attracted enough new clients to bring back my furloughed staff and employ more. We haven't stopped growing since. I have never been so driven and determined to grow my business. This isn't my first business and the thought of losing this one was the motivation I needed to seriously kickstart our growth.

Top Tips

My three top motivational tips when facing challenging situations:

1. **Keep up and you'll be kept up:** I'm a big fan of kundalini yoga and there's a saying, 'Keep up and you'll be kept up'. For me, it's a bit like compound interest helping to increase your savings over time. If you keep showing up and putting in the work, the energy created will increase the output and rewards.

   When you find yourself overwhelmed by the magnitude of a situation, break it down into smaller, manageable tasks. Focus on one step at a time, setting achievable goals along the way. By dividing the challenge into bite-sized portions, you can maintain a sense of progress and accomplishment, fuelling your motivation to keep moving forwards.

And if you want to try kundalini yoga, you'll find your physical and mental strength will vastly improve. There are a variety of free lessons online to check out, but I personally love Brett Larkin and am subscribed to her Uplifted membership.[19]

2. **Seek support:** You can't sit back and expect others to fix your problems, but that shouldn't stop you from reaching out for support. Surround yourself with a network of friends, family, mentors or colleagues who can offer encouragement, advice and assistance. Sharing your burdens and seeking guidance from others can provide you with fresh perspectives, boost your morale and remind you that you're not alone in your journey.

   Don't be afraid to ask for help – it's a sign of strength, not weakness. Consider joining a business mentoring group such as BiP100.[20] Chances are someone in the group has been through your situation or something similar before and can share how they got through it.

3. **Visualise your successful outcome:** What would be a great outcome? Maybe there are a number of potential favourable outcomes?

---

19   Brett Larkin Yoga: Uplifted, www.brettlarkin.com, accessed 21 July 2023

20   BiP100 Club, www.bip100.club, accessed 21 July 2023

Write them down and then close your eyes and play it out in your mind. Feel it as if it's really happening. You can practise the moment – even if you don't know how you're going to get there yet. Visualisation can help strengthen your belief in your abilities and create a mental roadmap for achieving your goals. By visualising success, you reinforce your motivation and inspire yourself to take the necessary actions to make it a reality.

By incorporating these tips into your approach, you can harness the power of motivation to overcome hurdles, achieve success and unlock your full potential in many challenging circumstances. So, embrace these strategies, persevere and let your motivation be the driving force that propels you to victory.

Alison Shadrack is the Founder and CEO of Adia PR, the PR Agency for disruptive entrepreneurs and thought leaders, helping entrepreneurs to build brand awareness and improve their own visibility, credibility and reputation. Her clients are regularly featured in the top tier of the media world, including *The Telegraph*, *Forbes* and Sky News and they're frequently winners of coveted industry awards.

Alison has been recognised as a leading PR expert by Enterprise Nation and Experian, who selected her as one of the Top 50 Business Advisers and Top 5 PR Advisers in the UK. Alison previously worked for Accenture in London, a property firm in New York and the European Commission in Brussels.

in www.linkedin.com/in/alisonshadrack

The Difference Between Wanting To Do Something And Actually Doing It

CHRISTOPHER SIGMOND

As I am sitting down to write this chapter on motivation, I am not feeling very motivated. I mean, I really want to do it, and when I was asked to contribute to the book, I felt very happy indeed. But right now, I feel a bit – demotivated. So, I thought rather than telling you about motivation from some kind of theoretical perspective, I would share my motivation process as it is right now, about getting into the flow and into doing what I want to do. Because the interesting thing is that there is a difference between *wanting* to do something and *feeling motivated* to do it. (And once the feeling is there, then the doing is easy.)

When I want to do something, there is a decision, a firm resolve, a conviction that this is in line with my interests. However, in order to overcome the inertia and get to the actual doing, something more is required. So, I go to the kitchen and find myself a nice, red, organic apple, that I am now crunching away at. I like the taste, the texture, the fragrance, the juiciness – the full 'apple-ness' of this experience, and that makes me happy. Being happy is a good stepping stone towards motivation. It is all downhill from there. Well, not quite, but that felt like such a catchy phrase, I wanted to say it. Actually, being happy is only a part of the puzzle, albeit an important one. There are certainly other feelings that can motivate, such as fear, anger or even grief. But I find happiness to be the most life-affirming and the least treacherous one, so I prefer to go for happiness. Of course, happiness, like all emotions, is transient. But so what? Life is changing all the time. That is a given.

By first getting happy and allowing myself to feel good, things flow naturally, seemingly without effort. My fingers are now dancing on the keyboard and I'm witnessing it. Such bliss.

Was it the apple that motivated me? Surely not. But the experience of the apple – indeed, the feeling of doing something nice to myself and exercising self-love – well, that goes a long way.

And now my son comes in and wants to play. Interruption alert!

– But wait, what if I welcome this as a stepping stone for the next step... which I do... We play pirates and juggle, and meanwhile, my mind is processing the text that I have written and what might come next. Allowing the creative flow to come however it may. Accepting it all. Embracing, rather than rejecting. Surfing the waves that are presented to me, rather than trying to force something – something which is bigger and more powerful than me, anyway. And then, it just flows. The motivation has levelled up, and I am having fun at the same time.

Play is inherently mammalian and thus the simplest and most natural of activities – arguably what makes life worth living – and such an advanced form of living, as well. The highest state of being together with others.

– Have you ever seen children completely engulfed by play? Now that is pure motivation! So, what if we surrender to the moment and emulate that, 'Fake it 'til you make it', and when you are serious enough to play, you will find that it all flows. Perpetual flow.

And so, motivation is fully integrated and thus transcended to a point where the chasm between wanting and feeling is no longer present, but the two have merged and our doing and our being are but two sides of the same coin. A coin of immeasurable abundance that we can choose to receive with ever increasing gratitude.

CASE STUDY: A HOLISTIC APPROACH TO MOTIVATION

I work with intellectual, emotional, physical, social and spiritual perspectives.

Now, for each of these perspectives there is a positive and a negative motivating factor: One moves *towards* and the other moves *away from*.

The positive factor of intellectual motivation presents itself as curiosity – wanting to know more about something or someone – whereas the negative factor is the frustration of not understanding something or someone – leading to withdrawing from further investigation.

Emotional motivation in its positive factor has a warm fuzzy feeling of relaxation and safety, whereas its negative counterpart is fear, sometimes mixed with anger or grief.

The positive factor of physical motivation is pleasure in the body – something of which there are many versions – while its negative factor is avoiding pain.

On the social level of motivation, the positive factor is the wish to connect, and the negative could be phrased as not wanting to make a fool out of oneself.

Finally, spiritually, the positive factor is being a creator, ie, creating or being in the creative flow, and the negative is shutting down, becoming invisible or trying not to be in the way.

I grew up in a home which rewarded intellectual curiosity, so that comes easily to me, and I have certainly followed my curiosity throughout the years, whether pursuing academic studies, making career choices or in choosing whom to surround myself with. More often than not, this has meant trying new things, searching and finding, seeing things from different perspectives, making new connections or building structures in my mind.

Emotionally, my home was in an almost constant upheaval and fear was prevalent. This affected me in all the typical ways of fight, flight, freeze, fawn – or my latest addition: fidget. In some regards, I became almost paralysed. In others, however, I developed a proclivity to throw caution to the wind and run headfirst into uncertainty, into adventure. This has meant entering many interesting situations, some less safe than others... But I have got plenty of stories to share.

Physically, I have always been slim. As a child I was not particularly tall, but today I am close to two metres (6'4"). I tried going to the gym, but that failed to capture my attention. However, what I really like is dancing. This was not always the case – I remember with vague embarrassment how we were forced to learn some basic dance moves in school. It was when I went to Goa in my early twenties that dance opened itself to me, at a rave party on a beach. Ever since, moving the body freely to music has been my preferred way of physical exploration.

Socially, I used to be quite shy. Actually, I still am, but very few people notice, since I have spent so many years learning to be extroverted. This is a mixed blessing, because even though this has helped me in a world that rewards extroversion much more than introversion, a part of me, a very valuable and sensitive part, was relegated to the sideline for a very long time. Lately, however, I have been seeing a rise of this all-but-forgotten side, and what a boon it is to bask in its sublime glory. And I am having so much more fun. Because I am me. And I am kind of a fun person to be around.

Spiritually, there is something really beautiful about creating and playing, which are more or less the same thing. This is really at the core of what I value and cherish the most, whether it be playing music alone or with others, playing with friends, small or big, or just the spontaneous creative flow in a really good conversation. Listening to words that have never before been spoken, whether from my mouth or someone else's. Such bliss!

Top Tips

1. Embracing abundance

The question of motivation usually comes to the fore when motivation is perceived to be wanting. This means that the starting point is one of lack, which is not a good place. In fact, it is a really bad place to start doing anything, because that sense of scarcity will have an adverse effect. However, by shifting to a sense of abundance, we are already on a roll. And being on a roll is good for motivation

– arguably, it is motivation in action. So, the question then becomes how to get to a state of abundance, and one answer is through gratitude. By practising being grateful for what one already has, whether physically, intellectually, emotionally, socially or spiritually, a sense of accomplishment ensues. It can feel like half the battle is already won, which means a flying start.

Another way to get to a mental state of abundance is by giving something away. Ideally, by giving away that which one wants to receive. This might sound like a contradiction, but it really works. Imagine that you want to feel abundant around money. Then a good way to get started is to be generous with the money that you do have towards someone who is in an even more precarious situation than yourself.

A third way to feel abundance is by simply opening up to receiving. Now, this is probably the hardest and most advanced of the three, because it really requires you to change your perception completely. You might not even see that there is anything to receive, so how can you be open to that? Yet that is exactly what you can do. It might help to start with something that is most likely abundant where you are, like air to breathe. By cultivating a receiving mindset around the air, and appreciating that which is received – gratitude helps here as well – you will soon see other wellsprings, because abundance is real everywhere, and there is plenty to receive if you just open up to it. NB, this is *not* about taking what you want, but rather about receiving that which is freely given, which is a very important distinction!

2. **Motivational shifts**

A second way to get motivated is to make a motivational shift between perspectives, eg, from an intellectual to a physical perspective. So, if you feel demotivated, you might leave the computer and eat a delicious fruit, or agree to end a meeting early and immerse yourself in something creative like playing music, painting or sculpting.

3. **The Stepping Stone Technique**

Third, there is something that I have named 'The Stepping Stone Technique'. In this one, you move from where you are to a place that makes you feel good, even if it is seemingly contradictory to where you want to go. The point is that by doing something that feels good, you cultivate a very important part of motivation – the 'feeling' aspect. And by immersing yourself and really enjoying this feeling, by going to a place that you feel motivated to go to, you gain momentum. This momentum can then be utilised to propel you towards the next step.

Christopher Sigmond grew up in an intellectual and dynamic home, and therefore learned to listen and understand early.

After acquiring degrees in philosophy, engineering, law and technology, with higher studies in music, group psychology, languages, leadership and more, an eight-year career in railway engineering, lots of dance, several long voyages and many other things, he started the company SiriusSounds AB in 2020, offering his services as a Personal Philosopher and Business Philosopher.

He works in a multi-disciplinary way that includes intellect, emotions, body, relations and depth, and helps individuals and organisations to understand and take the next step in their development.

Christopher, aka The Listening Philosopher, is available worldwide for those brave enough.

More about Christopher and SiriusSounds here:

🌐 https://siriussounds.com

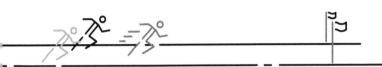

Motivation Is The Driving Force Behind Our Thoughts, Actions And Behaviour

JANE THOMAS

Motivation derives from the Anglo-Norman term 'motif', which is translated as 'drive'. Our motivations are our inner drivers that determine how we feel and *why* we do what we do, giving us the energy and enthusiasm to pursue our goals and aspirations.

When individuals clearly understand their 'why', they are more likely to stay motivated and committed to their goals, even when faced with challenges and setbacks. In contrast, motivation can wane when the 'why' is unclear or absent and goals may be abandoned or left unfulfilled. Understanding and clarifying the 'why' behind our actions and goals is essential for sustaining motivation and achieving success.

There are different types of motivation: intrinsic motivation (driven by internal factors such as personal interest or enjoyment) and extrinsic motivation (driven by external factors such as rewards).

Our motivational drivers are the forces that push us forwards, keep us focused on our goals, and drive us to take action, such as personal values, beliefs, desires and aspirations. They are essential for success because they give us the energy to overcome obstacles and achieve the highest level.

Reasons why motivational drivers are crucial for success:

1. **Increased focus and direction:** Strong motivational drivers give us a clear sense of purpose and direction. We know what we want to achieve and are willing to do whatever it takes to get there. Focus and direction are critical for success because they help us stay on track and avoid distractions that might hinder our progress.

2. **Greater resilience and determination:** Motivational drivers provide us with the resilience and determination we need to overcome obstacles and setbacks. Resilience and determination are

essential for success because they help us bounce back from failure and recover quickly. When we face challenges, we are more likely to persevere if we have a strong motivation driving us forwards.

3. **Improved performance and productivity:** Motivational drivers can significantly impact our performance and productivity.[21] When we are motivated, we are more likely to work harder, be more creative and come up with innovative solutions to problems. This increased performance and productivity is critical for success because it helps us achieve our goals more quickly and efficiently.

4. **Greater satisfaction and fulfilment:** We are more likely to feel a sense of satisfaction and fulfilment when we achieve our goals. Satisfaction and fulfilment are essential for success because it helps us stay motivated to continue to strive for excellence in our lives.

Motivational drivers are also closely linked with physical and mental wellbeing, which can have a significant impact on an individual's motivation.[22] When an individual's physical or mental health is compromised, it can lead to a lack of motivation and reduced overall satisfaction with life.

---

21   J Sale, *Mapping Motivation* (Routledge, 2015)

22   J Sale and J Thomas, *Mapping Motivation for Leadership* (Routledge, 2021)

Decreased productivity and reduced ability to concentrate potentially lead to stress, anxiety and possibly depression. When an individual is physically unwell, they may feel tired, lethargic and have a general lack of energy with physical symptoms like headaches, fatigue and body aches. This may affect their motivation to engage in physical activities, work, or even basic daily tasks, leading to poor mental health which can impact in several ways.

Maintaining high levels of motivation requires caring for both physical and mental wellbeing. To achieve this, it's essential to prioritise healthy eating, exercise and sleep, which form the foundation of overall health, linking to Maslow's Hierarchy of Needs. It's crucial to maintain a balance between physical and mental health to ensure optimal motivation levels.

Understanding what fuels and drives you is essential to achieving peak performance in your personal and professional life. When you clearly understand your motivations, passions and values, you can channel them into your work and tap into a powerful source of energy and focus. You can better align your goals and actions with your core values and passions. When you are engaged and motivated, you are more likely to stay committed to your goals, even when faced with challenges or setbacks.

Moreover, knowing what your driving factors are allows you to prioritise your time and energy on tasks that are most aligned with your goals and values. This leads to greater efficiency and effectiveness, as you are focusing your efforts on activities that are most important to you and your success.

When you have a clear sense of purpose and motivation, you are more likely to be resilient in the face of obstacles or failure. You are better equipped to learn from setbacks and use them as fuel to keep moving forwards towards your goals.

By understanding our personal motivational drivers and harnessing their power, we can unlock our full potential and achieve success in all areas of our lives.

But do we know what motivates us?

Motivational Maps are an ISO-accredited proofing tool. To create a motivational map, the participant completes a questionnaire. Based on nine motivators, each motivator represents a different driving force. Each one has a unique combination of motivators that influence their behaviour and decision-making. The answers are analysed and identify the individual's motivating factors, along with targets and strategies for reaching future goals. The participant will receive a multi-page report which will be explained and delivered by an accredited practitioner to allow them to gain the most from it.

Once completed, Motivational Maps provide individuals with a visual representation of the ranking order of their motivators, with an explanation of what each factor represents and, more importantly, whether these motivators are being satisfied. This information can be used to identify areas for development, create actionable goals, improve performance and productivity and maintain wellbeing.

CASE STUDY: MOTIVATIONAL MAP

The case study involves a Deputy Headteacher who is off sick with anxiety and depression and is considering leaving the teaching profession. Despite her love for teaching, she does not want to move into a Headship and would like to set up a pastoral care service for new teachers entering the profession. However, her family and partner are pushing her to apply for a Headship, leading to panic and anxiety attacks.

After completing a Motivational Map assessment, the Deputy Headteacher's overall motivational score was 68%, with her top three motivators being met in her love for teaching. However, she felt trapped in her current role, leading to clinical symptoms that incapacitated her ability to focus and think clearly. The assessment also revealed that her two dominant areas were the Growth cluster, where she wants to have a purpose and make a difference, and the Relationship cluster, where she enjoys giving pastoral care to teaching staff, children and parents. The Achievement cluster was the lowest. She had previously been a high achiever through her studies, but it was not as much of a driver currently, as confirmed by her attending the Headship training programme.

The Deputy Headteacher was considering three options: finding another job outside of teaching, taking a four-month period off sick until the end of the term to consider her options, or setting up a company with a strong connection to pastoral care and mentoring teachers. The Motivational Map confirmed that setting up a company would be her driver to stop the anxiety and panic attacks, thus giving her a structure to focus her current level of 68% motivation on starting her entrepreneurial journey of setting up a company to support teachers in their role.

The outcome of the case study was achieved in just one two-hour session. By helping her identify underlying factors affecting her wellbeing, the Map provided valuable insights that may not have been immediately obvious. By understanding these factors, individuals can take steps to address and channel their motivational energy in a more productive direction.

The case study highlights the importance of understanding our personal motivators and ensuring that they are being met in our work and personal lives. When we are not channelling our motivational energy in the right direction, it can lead to dissatisfaction and even clinical symptoms. Using tools like Motivational Maps, we can identify areas where our motivators are not being met and make changes to ensure that we are utilising our motivational energy to align with our values, interests and goals. By leveraging our personal motivators, we can unlock our full potential and achieve success in all areas of our lives, providing insights for making positive changes and improvements.

Top Tips

Optimising motivation and performance can be a complex process involving various self-development factors and goal setting.

Placing the importance of setting specific, measurable and achievable goals helps you focus on what needs to be accomplished to provide a clear direction for performance and engagement. Goals should be challenging, but not so difficult that they become demotivating.

Ask yourself: how can I be more effective over the next six months? In reviewing your answers, what do you learn about yourself? Which of your self-suggestions seem most relevant and powerful? Is there a pattern in what they are? Are they tangible, intangible or development issues?

Feedback is vital. Investing in professional feedback such as training, coaching and mentoring can provide valuable insights, helping individuals identify areas for improvement and develop strategies to overcome them. Ask yourself: where do you get your feedback?

Being an entrepreneur, coach or manager can be lonely and isolating. If what motivates you is being with people, then look for collaboration. Collaboration can lead to improved performance by leveraging your strengths with the sharing of knowledge and skills.

Do you need recognition and reward for achievements to help motivate you to perform at your best? Rewards can be financial or non-financial, such as public recognition, additional responsibilities or increased autonomy.

How does your environment affect your motivational levels? Consider physical, social and personal factors and organisational culture. Your environment can have a significant impact on your motivation levels. Creating a supportive and encouraging environment that fosters motivation and productivity is important. Where do you get your motivational support?

In summary, my top three tips are:

1. **Set achievable goals:** The most effective way to stay motivated is to set achievable goals. When you set a goal that you can realistically accomplish, you feel a sense of accomplishment and are motivated to keep going. Break down your goals into smaller, manageable steps to make them more achievable.

2. **Celebrate your successes:** Celebrate your successes, no matter how small they may be. Take time to acknowledge and celebrate each success. Recognising your accomplishments helps to reinforce positive behaviour and builds momentum towards achieving your goals. Share these successes with colleagues.

3. **Find inspiration:** Find sources of inspiration that will help you stay motivated. Read

motivational books, watch inspiring videos or talk to someone who inspires you. Surround yourself with positive people who support and encourage you. Find role models who have achieved what you want to achieve. Join a networking community and be an active participant. Share your knowledge and experience, and be open to learning from others. You can build valuable relationships and grow both personally and professionally.

By implementing these strategies, you can optimise your performance, improving productivity, efficiency, job satisfaction and accelerated motivation.

Jane Thomas is a highly skilled trainer and founder of Premier Life Skills, and is passionate about providing the highest quality training. As one of just five Senior Licensed Practitioners of Motivational Maps across the globe, she specialises in using an ISO-accredited tool that measures levels of motivation and satisfaction. Her company is an accredited centre for the Level 5 Diploma in Mental Health and Wellbeing Awareness.

Jane's focus is on creating healthier workplaces. With her extensive experience and expertise, she is an excellent choice for organisations seeking to invest in their employees' health and wellbeing and enhance their team's performance, productivity and motivation.

To learn more about Jane's training services or to complete a complementary Motivational Map:

🌐 www.premierlifeskills.co.uk

in www.linkedin.com/in/janepremierlifeskills

Motivation Is Easier When You Feel In control

ROBIN WINNETT

A key question to ask young and old alike is: how can you engineer your business life where you have a much greater chance of being in charge of your own destiny?

For me, and I suspect for many people attracted to read this book, the best way is to work for yourself rather than others.

This has always been sound advice in my opinion and even more so in today's world. Powered by ever-increasing computing processing power, AI, Blockchain, IoT, always-on quicker internet connection and substantial developments in all sciences, the world we now live in is an exciting place to be where the speed of change is increasing – exponentially.

Why does it help if you work for yourself? I include both business owners and self-employed in that statement. Answer: it is far easier to make adjustments to the direction of your career and personal life – a bit like steering a ship across an ocean, even the smallest adjustments will result in a significant change in your final destination. The larger the organisation, the more risk you have of becoming a passenger rather than the skipper. Wouldn't you prefer to have at least a hand on the rudder? For example, how about aiming to be part of the leadership team of a small business?

Let's take a step back and consider what drives motivation. I'm a firm believer in Maslow's Hierarchy of Needs in which Maslow argued there are five different levels of need that drive motivation:

1. Physiological: Basic needs for human survival.

2. Safety: Protection from physical harm, financial stability. A sense of order and predictability.

3. Love and belonging: Social connections, friendships, romantic relationships. A sense of community.

4. Esteem: The desire for recognition, respect and status.

5. Self-actualisation: Fulfilment by realising your full potential. Making a difference.

Maslow argued that lower-level needs must be satisfied before you can focus on the next level.

From this, it follows that finding activities that deliver these higher levels leads to greater motivation, and can be sustained. Either this means finding work that achieves all five levels or something outside 'work'. The latter means engineering a life which allows you to devote time and energy without risking Maslow's lower levels, ie, your financial needs for the life you want to lead.

We are entering a period where disruptive technologies are creating exponential changes in our personal, and probably more so in our professional, lives. Doesn't it make sense to have more control over how rapidly you can adapt?

Being able to adapt quickly, I see the following benefits:

1. You are more likely to be in a position to take advantage of the opportunities that always exist in a changing world.

2. By adapting quicker, you will build up a much clearer picture of how and what you need to do

to become more fulfilled in your personal and business lives.

3. Clarity will bring greater motivation and, at the same time, lead to a more fun and fulfilling life along the way. Always remember, life is the journey rather than the destination.

4. When further change happens, as it surely will, you will become an expert at adapting. This is becoming a key skill in this industrial revolution.

I'm a half-glass-full type of guy, so while I do see quite a lot of choppy waters ahead, I do/must believe the human race will find a way to harness these technologies for a better future for the planet and the population of nearly eight billion people. Do you want to join me to help make that outcome more likely?

CASE STUDY: CLARIFYING MOTIVATIONS

There have been three stages to my business life, #no-idea, #some-idea, #I-have-a-plan:

#no-idea

I suspect like many young people, when I stumbled into my first real job, my main motivation was basic: earn some money and, in my case, a stop-gap until I got a 'proper job'. Computerising a fast-growing innovative music distribution company proved to be a wonderful apprenticeship. We were 'in-flow' or, using the sporting analogy, 'in the zone'. A tight bunch of people, all eager to support each other, all of us knew our roles and delivered against them. As work was fun and we had such momentum, we were all happy to over-deliver.

In seven short years, we went from under £1million to nearly £8million. A poor strategic decision by the MD, the majority shareholder, resulted in a sad end. However, I will never forget witnessing first-hand the exponential benefit when you have the right people in the right positions.

My main contribution was to design and build a number of software products that were recognised to be market leaders within the industry that included big players like Polygram, BMG and EMI.

#some-idea

In 1998, I needed to retrain and learn a software development language that used this new thing called 'Windows 3.1'! 'Only pay me if you like it,' was my compelling offer to a small-business owner. When my solution was shown to be significantly better than their current solution, I found that I had stumbled into having a client and owning my own business, especially when my application was expanded and adopted by the much larger arm of the company based in New York.

By April 2009, we had built up a team with a reputation for designing and overseeing the development of complex business systems, delivering them to a fixed-price budget and on time.

The effects of the financial crisis hit us and we lost 50% of our turnover in a 6-week period. Painful and expensive lessons followed and yet, in my view, ultimately led to clarity of what my motivations are and to finally have a plan to work towards. The fact I had married my wonderful wife, Jude, in 2005, was, and remains, a significant factor.

#I-have-a-plan

Every person is different, with different strengths and weaknesses. I get frustrated by TV programmes that give the impression there is only one type of entrepreneur, ie, you must be prepared to work eighteen+ hours a day/ seven days a week.

This advice, in my opinion, is suitable for less than 5% of the entrepreneurs I've met.

By the way, I love working to a non-moveable, tight deadline. We have had some of our best business successes delivering against some incredibly tight deadlines. My point is, ensure you are spending your time wisely and you are working long hours because you want to and there's a business need rather than a belief that you have to. Your motivation will increase when you do this.

Personally, I am far more effective when I have space to think. I believe this is true for the vast majority of entrepreneurs.

I am now a fully signed up member of the 'work smarter, rather than harder' club. Especially since 2012, I've built up my skills and toolset which I personally apply and encourage my clients to do the same. They are:

1. Application of the Pareto Principle (which states that approximately 80% of consequences result from 20% of causes) throughout all business activities.

2. Active use of subconscious thinking – the most productive form of 'work', and for strategic positions (CEO, Owner, Managers, etc), the most valuable.

3. A continuous improvement mindset. My company name, after all, is Kaizen Systems!

4. Helping a business recognise what is needed to become 'in the Zone' and the exponential benefits that brings.

5. A collaborative mindset – the future of business, especially SMEs.

Have I achieved Maslow's five levels of needs? No, I feel I still have a lot more to give, but I do have faith in my plan.

Top Tips

My best three tips for motivation:

1. **Have a plan:** What's your 'end game'? I mean when you're aged sixty and older. I know that's harder to do when you are in your twenties or thirties, but trust me, the longer you spend time thinking about it and the further ahead you look,

the more a consistent picture will form over time.

Ensure your career and business aspirations are closely aligned with your personal plan. Identify what sort of work you love to do – it's usually where you add the most value.

When would you like to be financially secure – so you can choose when to work rather than out of necessity. This will also open up more opportunities to spend time on activities where you make more of a difference.

All activities which result in higher fulfilment will feed your motivation.

Be active and take steps that move towards your long-term goals. Working to a plan increases your motivation to do the most important things to make your future happen.

2. **Reflect back:** Expect the plan to change, especially when you are younger. Embrace and enjoy the journey. Just recalibrate. See how your new thoughts affect your long-term goals and stages towards them and adjust accordingly.

As mentioned before, over time I'm sure you will start to see certain goals and aspirations solidify – both business and personal. This is where your motivation will increase, as you will have a far greater belief in your plan and a stronger desire to make things happen and know the steps to get there.

At times it will be hard, and for most, really hard. In those times, my best advice is to reflect back and reward yourself on how far you have come, how much you have learned and how much better you are at making the right choices to become successful.

When I say successful, I'm defining that far more broadly than monetary terms. Remember, it's your life and your rules. If you are driven to work eighteen hours a day, great – but never assume that determines you are a success.

3. **Get support and build and treasure your network:** The best part of business is the people, and at times they can be the most challenging. The better you become at identifying your perfect customer, your perfect business partner(s), employees and your support network, the more enjoyable the journey will become and the less it will feel like work. You will have a much better chance of getting your business 'in the zone'.

'It's not what you know, it's who you know' is more relevant today than it has ever been. Your network will serve you in two very important ways.

First and foremost, I suggest you treat business like a hobby and find other people that share your passion. Some of those will be your best support pillars, and you, theirs.

Secondly, in the increasing world of collaboration, having people who you truly trust to call upon for your own business, from your clients or other people in your network, is a wonderful way to contribute and bring more value.

Finally, take time to enjoy and celebrate the successes and learn from things that fail to work as well as you had hoped. After all, life is the journey, rather than a destination. Good luck!

Robin Winnett is a practical and proven Software Architect with thirty+ years of experience in delivering innovative business solutions across many different industry sectors. Robin's strengths include a collaborative and continuous improvement mindset coupled with a good dollop of empathy and common sense.

He adds the most value when working to give the best possible exit to mature successful businesses.

Usually, an ageing or legacy complex bespoke software system is in urgent need of an independent review and/or the business wants to scale.

Time spent working closely with a digital marketing agency and an accountancy practice ensures he can contribute to broader business discussions – eg, how best to maximise a business opportunity.

in www.kaizensystems.co.uk

⊕ www.linkedin.com/in/robinwinnett